SIOBHÁN CAMPBELI
at the Loreto Conve
began writing poetry
first published her wo
she began working in book publishing, first for Butler Sims and then
Wolfhound Press. She has been actively involved in various writers'
groups, including the Dublin Writers' Workshop, Voicefree and
Palmer's Circle. In 1992 she spent six months in New York, where
she performed her work in Sin É and the Nuyorican Poets Café on
the Lower East Side. Her work has been published in numerous
journals including *Cyphers*, *Orbis*, *Poetry Ireland* and the *Sunday Tribune*.
She lives in Dublin, where she is married with one daughter. *The
Permanent Wave* is her first collection.

The Permanent Wave

SIOBHÁN CAMPBELL

*For Patricia Shiel
with very best wishes
San Francisco, March 20th '99*

Siobhán Campbell

**THE
BLACKSTAFF
PRESS**

BELFAST

ACKNOWLEDGEMENTS

Some of these poems have previously appeared in: *Cyphers*, the *Irish Press*, *Orbis*, *Poetry Ireland*, *Quarry* (Canada), the *Sunday Tribune*'s 'New Irish Writing', *Writing Women* (special Irish issue), *Hard Lines 3* (Faber and Faber, 1987), *Between the Circus and the Sewer* (Dublin Writers' Workshop, 1988), *Pillars of the House – Verse by Irish Women 1690 to the Present* (Wolfhound Press, 1988), *Irish Poetry Now* (Wolfhound Press, 1993), *Ireland's Women: Writings Past and Present* (Norton/Kyle Cathie/Gill and Macmillan, 1994). Thanks to the Tyrone Guthrie Centre at Annaghmakerrig, where some of these poems were revised, and to the Department of English, Trinity College Dublin, for the workshop given there by Paul Durcan.

First published in 1996 by
The Blackstaff Press Limited
3 Galway Park, Dundonald, Belfast BT16 0AN, Northern Ireland
with the assistance of
The Arts Council of Northern Ireland

Typeset by Paragon Typesetters, Queensferry, Clwyd

Printed in Ireland by ColourBooks Limited

A CIP catalogue record for this book
is available from the British Library

ISBN 0-85640-572-8

for
Kevin Conmy
with much love

CONTENTS

III

IV

V

I

REPRISE

Someone on a platform or in a queue
gives a low moan, a sudden slip into sound
of their thought as it churns.
And we, standing there, feel the thrall,
hear the faint cry of the child,
see ourselves in our first hurt, the hard
clenched grip and the reprise.
Our fingertips tighten as if to push away pain,
as if we could dam runnels of fear.
Like a breath, we hold it to be sure that we can.
We look around to see who this is
that has sifted our morning with doubt,
a doubt that will hum in our day's hold.
But not one of the crowd stands out.

THE CHAIRMAKER

I have been tempted to rush the job –
to cut, not shave; to glue, not join,
but when I stand beside it
and it's a friend or when I sit astride
and it's solid as a past, then I know
I am right to bide my time.

When people ask me how, I say
'My lady knows, she bakes loaves of bread.'
I tried that too until she said
if I kept opening the oven door
her rise would fall.

So I went back out to my shed
and dreamt myself a piece of elm.
I watched its wave and fingered the swell
and started to work slow as you like
letting my bevel follow the grain.

But this straight back kept coming up long,
thinned as it came until almost a pole.
I kept going although it was strange,
honing the shaft and slatting the seat
which was high and tiny and more like a tray.

She came to me when the loaves were done
as if to make up for forcing me out.
She looked at it and her eyes were lit,
'A bird table! We can put it outside,
sit on your chairs and watch them sing.'
And eat your bread, I said (I felt obliged),
and that night was as good as it's ever been.

ARTISTE

He has been painting her for weeks.
The hair a particular challenge
with flow round the ears.
He decided to cover them in the end.
Then there's the mouth,
it's arching at him like a fish.
He has painted over it twice,
resisted the cherub solution
but damn those lips! It's as if
she's eaten of his very art.

From where she sits, he reminds her
of a bird. Paintbrush poised,
he moves in little jerks.
He's grimacing today
as if he can feel talent rise
like sap in a tree.
Soon it will be time to send her home.
She'd much prefer to stay.
She would even do him free but she knows
it's not her place to say.

ID

Just when I think I have forgotten how to speak
someone will address me on the street.
They will ask me the way
while peering into my left eye
as if it were a map.
The loneliest of them will want to chat.
'You are often at this bus stop,' they will say,
dipping and twisting with shyness.

One girl was jigging up and down so much
I couldn't concentrate.
She wanted to time the next 46A.
I put out my hand to stop her
but she bent backwards,
started yelling from the ground.
The police are in there talking to her now.
I'm sure she's harmless
but they've asked me to stay,
probably to tell them all I know.

MINER

Once I used to dread the dark, the hardness,
how it could catch me watching my own smallness
or listening for fear (my second heartbeat),
always listening for the quiet crack of an opening
or the low rumble of stone.

We believed that we lived on the brink of the terrible,
toughened with the strength of overcoming fear,
and every month brought gories from South Africa –
of parallel collapse, of poorly slatted shafts,
of glory for our brothers underground.

Then we would go threading women in the town,
travel for hours in the hot jittering dust
to find that women only want a drunkard
or a clown and soon I began to stay behind.

They hate to call me miner as I have no miner's wife
and mothers fear to leave me with their sons,
but I go below where I can tell the light
that fades a lady blondly from my eye and where I know
a pure one when she draws me through the deep.

Sometimes I have been down so long
I yearn to sink inside her and be gone.
I know some morning I may be found out.
They will come upon me where I lie –
prostrate, naked, my fingers in her mouth.

ROMA SAYS

Let me lie on a dream sleep
slumber me mattress
under a real eider feather down
in a maple and cinnamon walled bedroom
used only for sleeping
and for no other purpose.

Then ask me to listen for rodents,
I wouldn't mind.

II

GRAN SEES DEATH IN A DREAM

The day after Gran had her dream
she gathered us all on the porch.
She wanted a promise we would pull the plug
if ever she was hooked to a machine.

She was scared they would keep her alive
until she shrank like a prune.
Nuns have only done all they can
when they know your money is gone.

None of us need feel bad, she said,
we could all have a hand on the flex.
By this act she need never be poor
and we could divide what was left.

She crushed ants into the porch
while her grip settled on our hands.
Each of us could feel her living will
waking in the cradle of our palms.

THE CONSTANT WELCOME

The constant welcome floors me.
I live here. I have arrived.
Yet still you cream me
with that smile.

I do not fight,
you'd twist my words to please.
I cannot go,
you'd follow if I leave.

But daughter,
do you know what I can hear
when your eyes are widening
as they want to close?

I can hear
the little scrape of hate
edging the high notes
of your voice.

THE PROMISE

Do not think I like to watch you
wearing thin, daughter.
Pocked and scarf red
you look the part.

You carry your duty like a flame
and leave me asking
what it is that I must do
to put it out.

But of this, daughter, be assured –
if ever you use me
to explain your lacking life
I will name you as the fraud
you really are.

BURN

Now the candle is forever lit,
a perpetual reminder of my effort
to make Christmas from an ugly plastic globe.
Instead I made your house *a tinker's caravan*
and your window shine *like a whore's beacon*.
I knew the small white candle cased in red
was some attempt to salve the way we lived,
ready to discard immediately your anger flared –
your bitter mouth flicking its tight line
to a skewed smile and back, so quick
you'd hardly think its heat could still be felt
or that the breath of pain between your words
would serve to feed the flame for years.

THE TWENTY-FIRST

I realise how this night will be used
for acting Grandma with the golden past
when she wants to photograph the birthday feast
before the guests arrive.

She has always retold my life,
run it at a pace it never found,
changing the detail as it suits,
making me the heroine or clown.

And I have listened to the family script
until through dropped word and held look
I caught the false,
drew myself a tracing of the truth.

'What are we doing it for if not for memories?'
She holds out the camera. I refuse.
The colours slide beneath her party face.
No child of mine would ever be so used.

I leave her in the kitchen with her feast,
holding the camera to her breast.
She at fifty at my twenty-first,
something between us beginning to reverse.

MY SISTER'S GIFT

This dictionary delighted my extravagance.
I bought you the deluxe, with thumb index,
to find you had already purchased.
You told me that I should have noticed.

I wanted you to take it from me
if only to acknowledge my intention,
to say that you would swap me yours
or just to read the dedication.

But I said nothing and you could not tell
this small twist of our linked tale,
like all the times I've watched you courting pain
while I have fought against my urge to warn.

One night late, I heard you propose
that limits of language are the limits of our world.
I thought about the dictionary I use, its wish
that you may always find just the right word.

GRANDMOTHER'S MIDSUMMER NIGHT

The night that Gran drank her perm money
she came down when everyone else was in bed
and laid her arms along the kitchen counter,
to feel the coolness, she said,
like a marble altar.

She had often thought during mass
of what it would be like
to lie flat on the altar,
naked to the Lord,
nothing between them but a nave of saints
that would shatter in mosaic when he came.

And why the surprise? she said.
Are you not of me as much
when you move your lover in your bed
as when looking back
you make of this night
my permanent wave?

THE LONG BACK

for my father

I thought I should have something of you,
a phrase I could hold on my breath,
an image that could be reused.
I knew it must have your accent, that
northern lean, that conscious bittering,
a sense always of what's at stake.

What I found was in among my limbs.
The Campbell wrist, its double-jointed turn,
my nails with their white flecks –
a lack of calcium, you would observe –
and my long back, this perhaps is it,
you told me it was just like yours.

This was the back you used to model new sweaters,
neck to waist in knitting pattern photos.
It became your chat-up line at parties –
holding your stomach in,
'Would you believe this was a model bod?'
You knew how to enjoy your headless fame.

Perhaps if I build my back to strength
I might feel the muscle as you felt,

invincible in aran or the best chenile,
rippling in pure lamb's-wool.
The knowledge could help me to forget
that this back kept you upright

even while your heart was giving up.
I would use it to suppress that view I never saw
but know; stunned by aneurism in your bed,
the book dropped open by your side,
a dark green V-neck on you that you had for years,
its folds subsiding as you cooled.

MASSY WOOD

I see you sitting beside a lamp made of leaves,
its base a lily, petalled flutes its globes,
in each a bulb. A greeny light
with a tinge of orange falls on the blank book
as you write in intermittent days,
sometimes recording a bird or a tree,
the way a hoarfrost remains
under a weak winter sun before the year turns.

When I show you that painting of the girl in red
through the leafless wood, your recognition
runs my spine. I can feel us slide
to a sadness and a warmth that is myself,
who today I may have met in that wood
where light through trees shows us
the aura of themselves and us walking
as if we were some of the belonged.

MY FATHER TEACHES ME TO MAKE
    SCRAMBLED EGGS

Take three eggs and a good-sized solid bowl.
Crack them in turn against the edge
and let their insides fall. Once open
they cannot be recalled. Like watching
the slip of your own fate beyond your reach –
happens for the first time about your age.

Mix them together, white and yolk,
self and the wish to be other.
Beat them with a fork against
the side. Don't worry about how hard,
a lather is good. The tougher the beat
the better the scramble will rise.

Put on to a hot pan a knob of butter,
a little milk and a darn of cheese.
These will sweeten the rawness as it cooks.
Swozzle the eggs around, no comfort
to be allowed; their function is bought
entirely when they're laid.

Serve when a yellow mass on buttered toast.
Makes the ideal after-funeral feast.

LEGACY

I

Going north meant Opal Fruits and Aztec bars,
things we couldn't get down south,
the thrill of secret cameras at the border
and the smell of ham in my grandmother's house.
Dad would skip tea, sitting in the car
where I ran once to get away from china dogs;
a shuffle of magazines into a paper bag –
had I really seen a bare bum in a tyre?

Later when I found them in his bedside drawer,
stories of caning set in schools or parties where
girls were made perform, my wetness drew me
and following the rhythms, I learned how to move.
Soon I knew *Playboy* had too much text on cars,
Hustler was more daring, written to arouse; two men,
one woman or the innocent's new job,
who will have her, she's wide open for the taking.

II

I took my fantasies from what you chose,
*Schoolgirl Susan Spanking, Debbie All Alone
in Summer.* I felt the hold of the observing eye
and learned the tone of the intimate narrator.

Lying on your bed, one ear attuned to anyone
returning home, I found new words for things
I had not seen; spunk and cock, jism and cum,
clit was a place I was not sure I'd been.

Weeks of waiting after you'd been north
would culminate in finding what you'd brought.
By now I could create a froth, summon
a spring, dive a deep river in my brain.
These rhythms I had learned to sing:
cunt becomes liquid, lips I have four,
my mouth devouring, nipples stand and stare,
the lightest flick from a wet finger and I'm there.

III

Then you produced a cutting on the white slave
trade to chasten me before I left for France.
On the back was a sliver of brown leg.
Here was headlined 'harems for sheiks
where young girls are kept against their will'.
Did the rest go on to make their abuse a thrill?
You saw that I knew what it was from.
You'd blown your cover in order to warn.

I left your drawer alone but what I read survived.
The cool onlooker through the two-way mirror
still arrives to speed my loving on as if
I'll never have the time. I want to shut it down,
to be wordless in my wonder or dream a new
theme from my own gender. But it's too late.
These riffs by now are mine. You helped to make
the lover I became. I am what you and I have known.

III

PICTURE PERFECT

Claiming the shady spot beneath the tree
with my guitar slung on its woven band,
I came, although I hardly play,
to test the image at first hand.

Now they join me one by two,
recognition leads an urge to bond.
I feel obliged to strum the 'Four Green Fields',
hoping I can hold the chord.

Thankfully they drown the need.
Straining, their raucous voices rise
as if in loudening they will reach the real,
as if it would evade them otherwise.

TESTING THE GREEN

You know that conversation you have
in the middle of the night
when the hotel porter is still serving
about who is more Irish than whom.
It begins with where you are from
and if you remember the '54 final
when Bannon's goal was disallowed.
Then whether you've milked by hand
or saved turf
or lapped hay into the night,
and used you serve mass?
With the last drink, you discuss that wrench
you feel when you hear James Galway
piping from a bar in New York or Perth
and you try for the words of 'The Croppy Boy'.
Once you've that sung there's no more to be said
but there's always one who wants the last word –
Ah, but did you have to walk
the five long miles to school
in the possing rain in your bare feet?

ANTRIM VIEWS

A girl lies in a field in the sun.
Leaves jitter beneath a spider's skip.
Above, a helicopter spins.
Webbed in, a fly pulls leave to wing.
Blades of clover reach in the warmth.
The girl in the field in the sun lies still.
Freckles open her everyday face.

Colours flatten, settling into hue,
drying from the outside in.
I realise that looking on, nothing is the same.
The moment steals the blood that curls
my liberal tongue. Jesus, Mary and Holy
Saint Joseph. I find myself praying
like a good Catholic girl.

On seeing a painting by Dermot Seymour:
Lysander over Ballymacpherson, County Derry

COUNCILLOR

He's a man that is marvellous at a mart,
can spy a sale from fifty yards.
A wadge of paper flapping in his hand,
there's always something special on his mind.

He fights to keep the plant that feeds the town,
holds meetings on the grant for sodden land.
At mass he's always half a prayer ahead
and afterwards he waits to meet the crowd.

He had Flynn's lane tarred to the back field
and a right of way kept over the stile.
Some say it was there he turned Flynn's daughter
the summer she finished with school.

He's the one that's tipped for the top,
we'll see him in Government yet.
A da's blind eye means a lot to him.
He'll earn whatever he gets.

ECONOMISTS

The economists are in bloom.
A long-lasting variety, perennial,
they will outshoot
unless kept carefully pruned.
The buds of promise but no seed,
the flowers that only last a day
or just until a change in weather
when the wind makes them blow
the other way, all the other way.
Bare again, thinking of a new colour.

THE AUCTIONEER

Passing them on the street,
she wonders if young boys
can see her shape
through a wool skirt.

Maroon, she thought,
was suitably mature.
Too short to be the fashionable length
but wide enough
to make long strides
and keep apace
with the longer-legged male.

Her tights are sheer,
suggest the other interests
she might have
besides being
a lady auctioneer.

And little do the young boys know,
her heart is cased in topaz brown
and blue tongues burn her
in an occult fire
when she makes love
alone.

ANTRIM BOARDERS

We used to meet
behind the science lab
where you went to smoke
and I went to read.
You named me Red.

They voted me
boy most likely to succeed
three years in a row
but then you skipped a class
and won because the lads were afraid.

And when we were left in Belfast
to make our own way home
I slid in with the post on a train.
But you told some republican Prod
that your granny was raped by a Brit
and arrived back in her Model T Ford
with your belly full of cream.

Once after science you showed
how you wore nylons
under your trousers

and I got a thrill.
Afterwards, I knew
you wouldn't meet me there again.

I've heard you are in London now
in a suit by day
and a skirt by night.
I wonder have you heard
that I am still called Red
or if you have guessed
that I never came out.

ELANA

Why does it darken Elana's face to bleed
when it is painless and in secret
and prepares her to receive?
Is she from where it was held
that only Satan could bleed without a wound?

Perhaps she knows that in Japan
they hang an orange hand on windscreens
of articulation to wave from women truckers
a warning in libation.

Or else she's remembering that hand
reaching from behind and through the crowd
while they listened to a street musician.
He found no warm chasm, index finger poised
met only a tough cushion and recoiled.

Elana is wondering how he felt.
Did he think of his mother draped in light
and ask had his father been betrayed,
did he curse her as a bitch in his disgust?
Yet, smiles Elana, it is probably
the closest to woman he will ever get.

Elana carries with her all the ways
that women named their ragging to the world –
the curse, the visitor, their Aunty Maud.
Elana keeps hers darkened in her eyes
although she knows it is, as moon and tide,
a simple part of life as it unfolds.

PLAT DU JOUR

Every day she chopped vegetables for their meal,
onion and carrots, sweet pepper, chilli and herbs.
Afterwards her fingers would smell of the roots.
Garlic would seep from her pores
when she lifted her hands to wipe her face.

Every day she chopped vegetables for their meal.
They would eat couscous, lasagne, pies. Sometimes
she overcooked or singed the edges on the pots.
Then their chiding would unroll, one off another,
and on bad nights she would cry.

The knife she used to chop herbs fine had a blade
so thin it beckoned. This day for ratatouille
she has washed and chopped for an hour and a half.
Her hands are an orchard of smell, a real kitchen garden.
Her fingers are spongy, pieces of parsnip ready to peel.

She takes the knife and being right-handed she knows
what she must do. That hand, dressed on the platter,
sliced through, finger by finger, a roulade
of onion flavour, garlic tips, artichoke palm.
Then she would never chop vegetables again.

IV

LA JEUNESSE TRIOMPHANTE

Rodin, 1894

He holds one hand wide-fingered at his spine,
the other resting lightly on the couch.
His shoulder blades are poised to pull him out
as if they could still raise him from her charm.
Her leg on his in case he tries to rise,
her hand curls the hair along his neck.
Both warnings are as gentle as the breath she blows
to divert the drip of sweat above his eyes.
He settles his knees so she won't slip
and still his hands are free.
It's up to her to make the final play
and now she does, reaching upward to his lips.
She is triumphant and controlling still,
she shifts so he will feel her nipples as they fill.

FUCHSIA

Fuchsia past its plum time
dribbling yellow streels,
yet the bee sinks a fur-brown head
in that purple flower.
A deep-seating suck, its back
quivers with success, then its sting
stiffens in the push for more.

I hope the flower
sets up her own enthrall
to use his deep to culminate her
and that she savours in the fragrant dusk
the soft cool as her best petals
fall in the after –
leaving her yellow stamens bare
to seed the coming year.

HILDA KNOWS

Her laugh is like one
she didn't mean to have.

Learning how
is still a surprise.

Sometimes the fake and the real
happen together.

Once she couldn't tell them
from each other.

That was awesome.

TOPPING STRAWBERRIES

Not even a ruddy stain remains
from these heartless beings.
They come already clean.
Leaving just a heap of pith,
some gritty seeds that graze
with the edge of stubbled chin,
a few hard green pellets, stunted;
the rest so smug in their perfection,
succulent, they pucker
as if they have always known
the feel of their own flesh
and are ready to kiss
their full-blown selves.

KITE

From flat to animal
shuddering alive
and rising on the beat
of an upswing.
Breathe its freedom
turn it through your thumb
flex its spine to the breeze
sweep until up to a full
height unroll oh!
Is this me, the quiet one
dark horse? A burst of
power in a field,
with bullocks running
frenzied in the next,
and all of us looking up and up.

BALLAD

We gave our horse
the run of the farm.
We let her wander
the fields.
After we ploughed
she clambered the soil,
loosening its folds.

At service time
she held herself proud
and ran then
as if she were the world –

as if she and the fields
and the raw earth
were in a conspiracy
of birth.

Mother and foal
we kept safe in the yard
as though what we feared
could come for her child.

And I can see her
as she came

to where we baled.
Her back thick with foam
her eyes rolling white –

the five-bar gate
dragging from her neck
snagging a leg
showing bone.

We found the foal
she had trampled
when all her demons rose.
It took us days to calm her.

We keep her for the cart
although her wind is gone,
and even blinkered
she shudders from the shaft.

SERVICE

Sweat whips his back.
His rearing lunge
a clatter of steel.
High whinnies
lewd the air.
Foam flies
in his stamping.

The mare in readiness
rolls her eyes.

I clamp my tongue
against the drumming
in my ears.

SUMMER LOVER

It's a pick them up
and get them down town
on the wide white coast
with a crop of tourists
snuggling into summer.

He loved with a high-profile
labour-intensive love,
deciding to declare
in a hotel bar
his urge to reach and touch.

He cuddled me
long and loud
on the leatherette seat.
Guests raised their heads,
pursing dry lips,
calling the waiter
who told us to quit it
or leave.

He was embarrassed for me
getting my coat,

his hand on my shoulder
grasping the bone,
imperative.

Sometimes I wonder
if he is still a summer lover
in that town
and whose June ear
he is settling into now.

THE MAN WHO WOULD NOT WED

Caught between a rock and a hard place
you chose to fly.
To fly on wings hand-made of lace.
Each curl and bobbin
a confection of restraint.
These wings took years
to cod and corner into shape.
You had minions, of whom you never spoke,
working in the half-light
somewhere above a steamy launderette,
making wings for you in the dark.
Why do you think
that they will take you to the sun?

AFTER

This is the edge of the dream
in the room.
I stand embossed
waiting to be touched.
Instead you frill me up,
talk to my eyes,
by the time you get there
I am fuss.

In the cool of my ear
I hear you lap.
I draw your name
then colour it out
until the letters squeal.

After drama I grow quiet.
But through the space
between my pores
I can feel the ruffle
of your being
unnerving
a corner of my room.

OPEN AIR

We come at evening for live Elgar,
hoping to capture something of what is lost.
Aware of this reason to be here,
we are discouraged by the microphones at first.
Once they clear, allegro can begin to thrill us
with the verve of violins.
But now our blood becomes a sweet to bugs.
Our slaps are not in time with anything.
We try to calm, to see ourselves
sunned and sitting upright on the grass.
But we must leave, the scratching is too much.
We rise and go to find a cool dark public house
where we can have a beer and start once more
rendering the evening with care.

CALMED

Lips that were rimmed with sand,
the last soft touch in our desert
are cool on my mouth.
Surely my eyes have darkened in their drawing in?
Blue they have pulled you down,
now I expect to see them dull to grey.

I am the cat on the hot car roof.
I am the blind spot in the corner of your eye.
I am the face in the curtain
that would turn your thought to flame.
When you walk the carpet in bare feet
you will feel the warm cushion of my thigh.

Yet it is true that soon all will settle.
Already my belly looks flat and white
as if it has not known your tongue buried,
delving to my back. But my smile
cannot reach the mark it used to make.
It quarries a shorter line in my tight cheek.

ONCOMING WINTER

Was it the birds that early left
or the cloud bank that curdled
on the hill or the tuberous plants
that sucked themselves in and away
that made me sure, so sure you would
be gone when the last bat hung
its blindness in my barn?

BY DESIGN

While we stippled
my bedroom walls
two flies chased their pleasure
dizzy on the smells
of paint and love.

Later you slept
while I heard the creature
humming her low aftersong
like my own.

You woke
as the buzzing failed
and said her partner's neat escape
proved missionary is best.

I felt aggrieved
as if I had been left
in a bind of love
with warm beige
tightening to a gloss
about my knees.

ELEVENSES

Mid-morning
when the post is finally cleared
after the first spate of phone calls
and shouting
when the day looks at last manageable
and I seem at last capable,

then only when I pause for my cold coffee
or to look up the number of a friend,
only then do I sense him
rising from me
his smell lifting from my hands
seeping from far beneath my pores.

I cup my hands and breathe him in,
even through soap and paper
he tunnels to me,
his smell expands me.

And in the next phone call
and in the next controlled confrontation
I will not let on
but I can taste him
on the tip of my organising tongue.

DRIVE TIME

He is fresh.
Some scent on cheek
completes the image of success.
The morning's his.

Shirt crisped about him
smoothed over a warm tum,
a nipple of memory
is brushed down.

I know what rivers
his chest in other times
can move, but now
he will face the working world

uniformed and blushing
in a lilac shirt, a crested tie
belies he knows my need
before it fires my eye.

By five, his stubble
rusts his chin.
A gathered brow
and little paper remnants

on his skin
now show his readiness.
His hair has lifted
from its place
and reaches for a touch.

Oh my chevalier!
Drive on home to me.

V

BIG JOHN'S TEARS FALL TO THE RIVER

You would always offer me a mug
hating the way my fingers surrounded your china.
You knew that being a cliché already
there was nothing to be done.
I wanted to tell you of my growing,
of that sudden sighting in the mirror –
but I am of this creature
and must love him for shelter.

In this town they don't expect to hear me speak
assuming some sort of generous simplicity
and you left because I failed to speak.
Now I am folded in lumbering despair.
Sometimes I wonder
did God have a hand in me at all
or was I fashioned
to make others raise a prayer?

CAFÉ PICCOLI

There he sits, his jaw uplifted,
breathing garlic as if it were his own scent,
sending it out across the café air
pungent and aware.

I could tease this man of the chiselled mouth.
Talking of his country,
rising his pride in the hot south.
I have taken note
his sweat is clean
and shining in his pores.
I would turn those statued lips to flesh
flooding out his poise.

Why do men die first
and leave us pining after them
like dogs?

The young man lowers his head and looks.
Perhaps he wonders what I'm doing here.
Is it my gold and double chins
that make him stare?
I've seen the gigolo before.
Could I be a customer for such a whore?

FARMER

At night it seems that nothing lives.
Without the low hum of the cooler,
the stamp and shuffle of beasts in the shed,
I might be deaf. I listen hard but cabbages
make no sound curling their close hearts.

Our yard was full of clang and batter,
the roll of steel churns along concrete
and the clatter of making butter, me by Ma's side
learning to hear the slide of curd from skim.

Now no din scatters the silence of my yard.
Birth pains no longer stretch the dry white shed.
Clean to its walls, it stores the pellets and pesticide
and sacks of fertiliser fill the stalls.

They came with their promises of grants.
We fought at the kitchen table and in the yard.
In the end the folks gave me my head.
Regret was left till after they were dead.

Nothing turned out like I thought.
I lie awake, hearing in my breath

the rhythm of how we used to work.
At the turn of night I fall asleep
to dream of a yard that sways with life.

CHANGE

The last calf
the last feed

the last flower of blood
in the kill shed

a lone bag of wormer
give it away

the yard clear
and scrubbed

smooth as the day
it was laid.

GRAPEPICKING

Secateurs sharpened, shoulders lower
furrow on furrow, over and over.

Wet and blue the ripe grapes fall,
slide as they land, skin on skin.

I pause to breathe the musky air
heavy with heat and fear of mould.

The farmer watches, acting bored,
counting buckets with a sodden stare.

Bending our backs beyond the need,
we stay until the night is blind.

As if we are not paid by weight
but measure what we feel is owed.

THE CAVE

The first to enter tracked his dog inside,
matchlit his wonder. We, however,
careful in the dripping wet
await the instruction of our guide.

She begins with the earliest formations
named as they dribbled from the porous stone.
We are amused by their preoccupations,
the praying hands beside the cuckold's horn.

'Sump,' she pronounces, pointing down.
'Flooded passage, underground well.
If you drop a coin you will not hear it
end its fall.'

She lists the crystals in a static fountain,
her education rounding out her vowels.
We think the frozen droplets are too beautiful
to warrant all these scientific names.

But at the crop of broken stalagmites
her words are enough to silence ours.
Five hundred years of growth was reaped
to sell as garden ornaments when food was scarce.

'Original life here was a blind spider
but man brought mutant fungi to their habitat.'
The guide snaps out her light.
'In this dark they had no need of sight.'

The blackness slides its wide arm close around.
We stand so still we hear the drip from calcite
fingers overhead. Relentless, the guide informs
they'll grow another inch before we're dead.

Unused to such a seamless dark,
our waiting edges with unease.
When finally she switches on
we are surprised to feel relieved.

Stepping up into the day that is ours,
we find ourselves unclenching in the sun;
the guide stands by as we emerge,
we wonder if she does the same with everyone.

We dare not ask.
Instead we tip her well
and follow her instructions
off the awkward hill.

SEVILLE CATHOLIC

To these dark shuttered sacristies
the women come who do the churchly duties.
They bring fresh laundry for the saints
and sew new finery for Easter ceremonies.
They seem to sing beneath their reverence –
We of the congregation are the few
who may touch Jesus in his nakedness.

The statues fitted out with clothes
are strange to us, coming from where
any drapery is modelled in the stone.
Some are elaborate in lace and velvet
and have underthings. We think it means
this faith is close to flesh and bone.

And when we see that woman, working
in a side chapel on her own, as she leans over
and fastens His linen surplice like a mother,
we see her pain and its remittance
gathered in this loving gesture.
And we feel the sway of her quiet fervour,
watching as if we've never touched its source;
the only residue, a feeling that it might be rude
to guess her hallowed words.

QUESTION

You tell me how you spend your days now.
Outside in the car listening to radio.
It's warm and your own place.
When you drive it is mostly to funerals –
one almost every week.
Once you were late.
You couldn't go in but had to wait till after,
when you'd queue to shake hands
and say sorry for your trouble.

You bought a new ice cream
for something to do – a Magnum,
it was cold and huge and delicious.
You sat in the People's Park on a felled tree
foregoing the bench as you would have when a boy.
Ants scurried in the wood folds,
helicopter seeds breezed down,
a late fly was busy in the fallen leaves.

All looked and sounded just the same.
It could be that you had never moved.
For a moment you saw the atoms
of the world in their ceaseless dance.

You understood. And then the vision closed.
Now you've begun to ask everyone you meet –
'Has there been a better time to be alive?'

OTHER POETRY TITLES

from

THE BLACKSTAFF PRESS

MODERN IRISH POETRY

AN ANTHOLOGY

•

EDITED BY
PATRICK CROTTY

In this ground-breaking new anthology Patrick Crotty
has assembled a stunning collection of over 250 poems to
represent the richness and diversity of the modern Irish
achievement in poetry.

From the gritty directness of Patrick Kavanagh to the more
formal cadences of John Hewitt and the sly lyricism of Nuala Ní
Dhomhnaill, this exciting new anthology demonstrates the
extraordinary scope and depth of poetry in Ireland since Yeats.
Major figures like Clarke, MacNeice and Ó Ríordáin are brought
into relationship for the first time, and the remarkable explosion
of writing north and south of the border in the last thirty years
is reflected in the work of poets like Kinsella, Heaney, Longley,
Durcan, Carson, Ó Searcaigh and Sirr. Women's poetry is
strongly represented by, among others, Eavan Boland, Medbh
McGuckian and Paula Meehan, and Gaelic verse by writers like
Máirtín Ó Direáin and Máire Mhac an tSaoi. All the Irish
language poems appear with facing translations.

Short biographical critical essays on each poet and a searching
and fair introduction make this an indispensable companion
for anyone wanting to experience the continuing challenges
and pleasures of one of the world's most vibrant
poetic traditions.

233 x 148 mm; 448 pp; 0-85640-561-2; pb

£14.99

AMERICAN WAKE

·

GREG DELANTY

'I sing now like the North American brown thrasher,
who at one point in its song orchestrates
four different notes: one grieves, another
frets, a third prays, but a fourth celebrates.'

Leaving home for America, Irish emigrants hold an 'American
wake', a gathering that is both festive and mournful. This new
collection from Greg Delanty articulates those complex emotions
through loving evocations of Ireland and nervy, excited
responses to the dislocating vastness of America. Whether
recalling a pubcrawl in the Bronx or the 'glorious banter' of his
Irish friends, he achieves a finely poised balance between the
lyrical and the conversational. Here the classic Irish themes of
exile and loss emerge as forceful presences, given fresh clarity as
Delanty traverses the physical landscapes of 'city, prairie, bush
or bog' and the internal landscapes of memory.

In the final section, he descends on a symbolic journey into a
Celtic 'realm of the dead'. Through the voices of Irish
mythological and literary figures – from Cú Chulainn and
Amergin to Patrick Kavanagh and Louis MacNeice – he
penetrates the 'lost centuries' of history, coming to terms
with the ghosts of Irish tradition in deceptively taut forms
and rhymes that are as witty as they are unexpected
and liberating.

'There is a fine balance between local colour and formal
correctness . . . readers will enjoy seeing familiar settings woven
into verse and emigrants will instantly recognise, in Delanty's
telling studies, the atmosphere of the Irish social scene
abroad . . . *American Wake* is rich in insights and images which
can be cherished individually or as part of a wave of
gravity that sweeps through its four parts.'
MICHAEL DUGGAN, *CORK EXAMINER*

198 x 129 mm; 72 pp; 0-85640-549-3; pb

£5.99

POETS FROM THE
NORTH OF IRELAND

.

EDITED BY
FRANK ORMSBY

'*Poets from the North of Ireland* presents some of the most
vigorous and challenging poetry written in English this
century. It not only reminds us of the importance of
Seamus Heaney's generation but allows us to trace the lines
of advance back to an earlier generation of John Hewitt and
Louis MacNeice . . . as a whole, it stands as an indispensable
guide to the remarkable achievement which has flourished in
the interstices of two cultures.'

OXFORD TIMES

'This is a treat – a collection of familiar and unfamiliar
Northern Irish voices; from Louis MacNeice to
Tom Paulin.'

OBSERVER

'*Poets from the North of Ireland* will continue to stand
unchallenged. It is an impressive general reader and
the perfect introduction . . . It should be
compulsory reading . . .'

FORTNIGHT

210 x 148 mm; 352 pp; 0-85640-444-6; pb

£10.99

A RAGE FOR ORDER

POETRY OF THE NORTHERN IRELAND TROUBLES

•

EDITED BY

FRANK ORMSBY

'. . . the Troubles have generated much of the most enduring art
to have come from the British Isles in the past quarter-century.
The strongest poets of Ireland, north and south, have
responded with a keenness of language and thought that should
be a model for civic culture everywhere. Scorning agitprop, they
have set aside nostalgia and escapism as well. *A Rage for
Order* . . . must be the most impressive verse anthology in
English for many years. Among over 250 poems from 68 poets,
it's hard to spot a false note or a dead idea.'

NEW STATESMAN

'full of superb work'

INDEPENDENT

'absorbing and unique . . . *A Rage for Order* is a welcome respite
from the statistics, the distant TV images and column inches that
have desensitised us over the years'

IRISH POST

'fine examples of the transmutation of outrage into art'

SCOTLAND ON SUNDAY

'In this anthology, there is no absence "from the frontier of
writing", no shying away from anger and injustice, bitterness
and sadness, perspective and analysis . . . like all quality
anthologies, this one wrestles at several levels, equally at home
on the school curriculum or the bookshelf of anyone who values
the challenge of words. Quite simply, buy it.'

IRISH NEWS

'an excellent collection of some of the finest contemporary
verse . . . essential reading for anyone with a serious
interest in modern Ireland'

THE TIMES

233 x 148 mm; 384 pp; 0-85640-490-X; pb

£13.99

THE COLLECTED POEMS
OF JOHN HEWITT

•

EDITED BY
FRANK ORMSBY

A POETRY BOOK SOCIETY SPECIAL COMMENDATION

'Ormsby's definitive collection, bringing together for the first
time all John Hewitt's published poetry plus a selection of
previously unpublished material, is a major contribution to the
understanding of this acclaimed figure in particular and
20th-century poetry in general.'
RICHARD PEARCE, *COVENTRY EVENING TELEGRAPH*

'Division, even in his early poems, is Hewitt's main theme. It
may be easy to over-Ulsterise this Protestant poet, but again and
again his poems circle, confront or try to bridge the severance
between the two Northern Irish communities.'
JAMES McKENDRICK, *INDEPENDENT*

'Hewitt's work is an unusual blend of analytic intelligence and
lyric intensity, by one who has harnessed the dry, laconic tones
of the Northerner for a lucid and compelling poetry.'
DECLAN KIBERD, *IRISH PRESS*

'Hewitt's voice goes on reverberating, sounding its distinctive
notes of sanity and decorum.'
PATRICIA CRAIG, *TIMES LITERARY SUPPLEMENT*

'As Europe painfully rearranges herself . . . Hewitt's big-
hearted, open-faced versions of regionalism, socialism and
atheism appear ever more relevant . . . The publication of this
volume is of historical as well as artistic importance.
Frank Ormsby, poet and scholar, has given of himself
with a generosity the great man deserves.'
MICHAEL LONGLEY, *FORTNIGHT*

210 x 148 mm; 784 pp; 0-85640-459-4; hb
£25.00

210 x 148 mm; 784 pp; 0-85640-494-2; pb
£14.95

DADDY, DADDY

·

PAUL DURCAN

**WINNER OF THE 1990 WHITBREAD POETRY PRIZE
SHORTLISTED FOR THE 1990 *IRISH TIMES*/AER LINGUS
IRISH POETRY PRIZE**

'. . . a startling, funny, critical and mesmerising book of verse, one of
the most purely enjoyable collections I've read for years . . .
Daddy, Daddy is a candid, subtle, daring book. And painfully funny.'
BRENDAN KENNELLY, *IRISH TIMES*

'Paul Durcan's . . . collection is as grandly challenging and
varied as one has come to expect from this bravely original poet
of *The Berlin Wall Café*. His poetry readings in this country are
sell-outs – to have heard him adds another pleasure to the
reading of his work – but the voice speaks clearly on the page
in poems of harrowing intimacy, politics and love.'
CAROL ANN DUFFY, *GUARDIAN*

Critically acclaimed for his vibrant and eclectic 'poetry of the
present moment', Paul Durcan is one of the most dramatically
intense of modern Irish poets. Drawing its strength from its
urgent treatment of a wide range of contemporary subject
matter, his poetry is also striking for the subtlety and
strangeness of its unique imagery.

In *Daddy, Daddy* Durcan pushes out in a radical new direction,
sounding new depths. Fusing the personal with the political,
his angry response to violence and oppression in poems such
as 'The Murder of Harry Keyes' and 'Shanghai, June 1989' is
incisive and humane. Here also are love poems of all manner
and kind; bizarre meditations on the nature of loneliness;
poems of celebration of writers and artists like Primo Levi,
Sylvia Plath and Paul Cézanne. And finally, in this collection's
last group of poems, he embarks on an exploration of his
relationship with his father, creating poetry that is
compelling in its probing artistry and painful honesty.

198 x 129 mm; 208 pp; 0-85640-446-2; pb

£5.95

RUINED PAGES

SELECTED POEMS
PADRAIC FIACC

•

EDITED BY

GERALD DAWE & AODÁN MAC PÓILIN

Subversive and unsettling, Padraic Fiacc's poetry is marked by
an unflinching engagement with the violent realities of Northern
Ireland. His staccato rhythms and sparse narratives are full of
taut, buried energies that convey a nightmarish vision of Belfast
and chart his disintegrating relationship with the world around
him. But behind the blasted city-scapes and shattered icons of
his poetry, there lies a gentle, tentative compassion and a
pervasive sense of lost innocence.

Ruined Pages celebrates the very best of Fiacc's poetry – ranging
from the tender lyrical simplicity of his early poems to the sharp
vernacular speech, macabre wit and brutal imagery of his later
work. Including *Hell's Kitchen*, a previously unpublished
autobiographical prose fragment, this definitive collection
presents the essence of the rawest and most intense poet
of the Troubles.

'Some would have us forget each horrendous event but Fiacc
would have us remember; not in a spirit of revenge but in a
spirit of unutterable compassion.'

PAUL DURCAN

'Authentic and moving poems made out of the chaos of
immediate history . . . a gentle, lyrical, reflective talent
compelled towards elliptical intensities of insight by
the violence in the streets.'

ROBERT NYE

198 x 129 mm; 184 pp; 0-85640-529-9; pb

£7.99

GRUB

•

MARTIN MOONEY

**WINNER OF THE 1994 BRENDAN BEHAN MEMORIAL AWARD
SHORTLISTED FOR THE
1993 RUTH HADDEN MEMORIAL AWARD
SHORTLISTED FOR THE
1993 FORWARD POETRY PRIZE FOR BEST FIRST COLLECTION**

Darkly comic, brilliantly allusive, elegiac – Martin Mooney's
Grub marks the début of an inventive and highly charged
imagination. Dealing with political hypocrisy, the nature of
creativity and love, his poems form a series of hard-edged
satirical parables exploring an eclectic range of subject matter,
including Anna Akhmatova's funeral, the Belfast shipyards,
body piercing and poll tax evasion.

Weaving a magical realist fable of a young Irish expatriate adrift
in Thatcherite London, *Grub*'s title sequence – with its cast of
corrupt policemen, malevolent ghosts and a rapidly
disintegrating band of punks and down-and-outs – draws
together elements as disparate as the *Marchioness* disaster and
the murder of Roberto Calvi to create a powerful narrative
constantly underpinned by 'the spiky friction of the
fantastic and the everyday'.

'Martin Mooney is a poet who can make a reader see the wild
extraordinary things that haunt the edges of our experience,
the extremity and the extremism of human action and suffering.
His fictions have the feel of history; he selects a viewpoint
without fuss or posturing and he keeps a steady eye, a sharp
tongue and an undistorted sensibility. The title sequence
of *Grub* is harshly elegant.'

EILÉAN NÍ CHUILLEANÁIN

'. . . a writer to watch. Energetic and satirical, the best of his poems
show a vivid imagination in tune with a street-wise intelligence.'

SEÁN DUNNE, *IRISH TIMES*

198 x 129 mm; 96 pp; 0-85640-500-0; pb

£5.95

ORDERING BLACKSTAFF BOOKS

All Blackstaff Press books are available through
bookshops. In the case of difficulty, however, orders can
be made directly to Gill & Macmillan UK Distribution,
Blackstaff's distributor. Indicate clearly the title and
number of copies required and send order with your
name and address to:

CASH SALES

Gill & Macmillan UK Distribution
13–14 Goldenbridge Industrial Estate
Inchicore
Dublin 8

Please enclose a remittance to the value of the cover price
plus: £2.50 for the first book plus 50p per copy for each
additional book ordered to cover postage and packing.
Payment should be made in sterling by UK personal
cheque, sterling draft or international money order, made
payable to Gill & Macmillan UK Distribution; or by
Access or Visa.

Please debit my Access* Visa* account
*Cross out which is inapplicable

My card number is (13 or 16 digits)

Signature

Expiry date

Name on card

Address

Applicable only in the UK and Republic of Ireland

Full catalogue available on request from
The Blackstaff Press Limited
3 Galway Park, Dundonald, Belfast BT16 0AN
Northern Ireland
Tel. 01232 487161; Fax 01232 489552